Jordan's Journeys

I0559720

A Friendship Beyond Words

an apraxia story

written by:
Jordan Christian LeVan

illustrated by:
Sydney J. Stone

Jordan's Journeys

A Friendship Beyond Words

an apraxia story

Illustrations by: Sydney J. Stone

"In a world full of bullies, be a Linwood."

Jordan has so many words inside -

waiting to come out.

It's the first day back at school,
and he feels both excited and a little nervous
about second grade.

He wants to ask a girl named Glenn on the playground
"Do you want to play?"

But when he tries to speak
"Puh... pl... uh..." the words
get caught.

Even though he knows them in his mind,
they try to stay hidden
as if playing hide-and-seek.

Jordan has something called "apraxia".

It's when the words on his mind can't find their way to his mouth

no matter how much he wants to say them.

He watches his classmates laugh and swing,
feeling like he's on the outside looking in.

With a sigh, he crosses his arms and sits on the bleachers -

watching from afar until class starts.

Still, he thinks to himself:
"I won't give up."

"I'll find a friend this year. I'll try my very best!"

Soon, the bell rings and he heads inside.

In class, the teacher calls on each child to introduce themselves.

Jordan waits - preparing to say his name.

But when it's his turn to speak, no sound comes out.

He sits back down, feeling sad even though he knows he tried.

The words are still inside, and he's waiting for someone who might understand him.

When lunchtime comes, he takes a deep breath
and sits near the kids in his class -

hoping today will be different.

He waves and smiles
as he places his lunch tray down,
thinking:

"Maybe I can use my hands
to say what I want to say!"

He taps on his tray and points at a classmate's sandwich, hoping to ask what they're eating.

But they don't understand his gestures, and soon they look away.

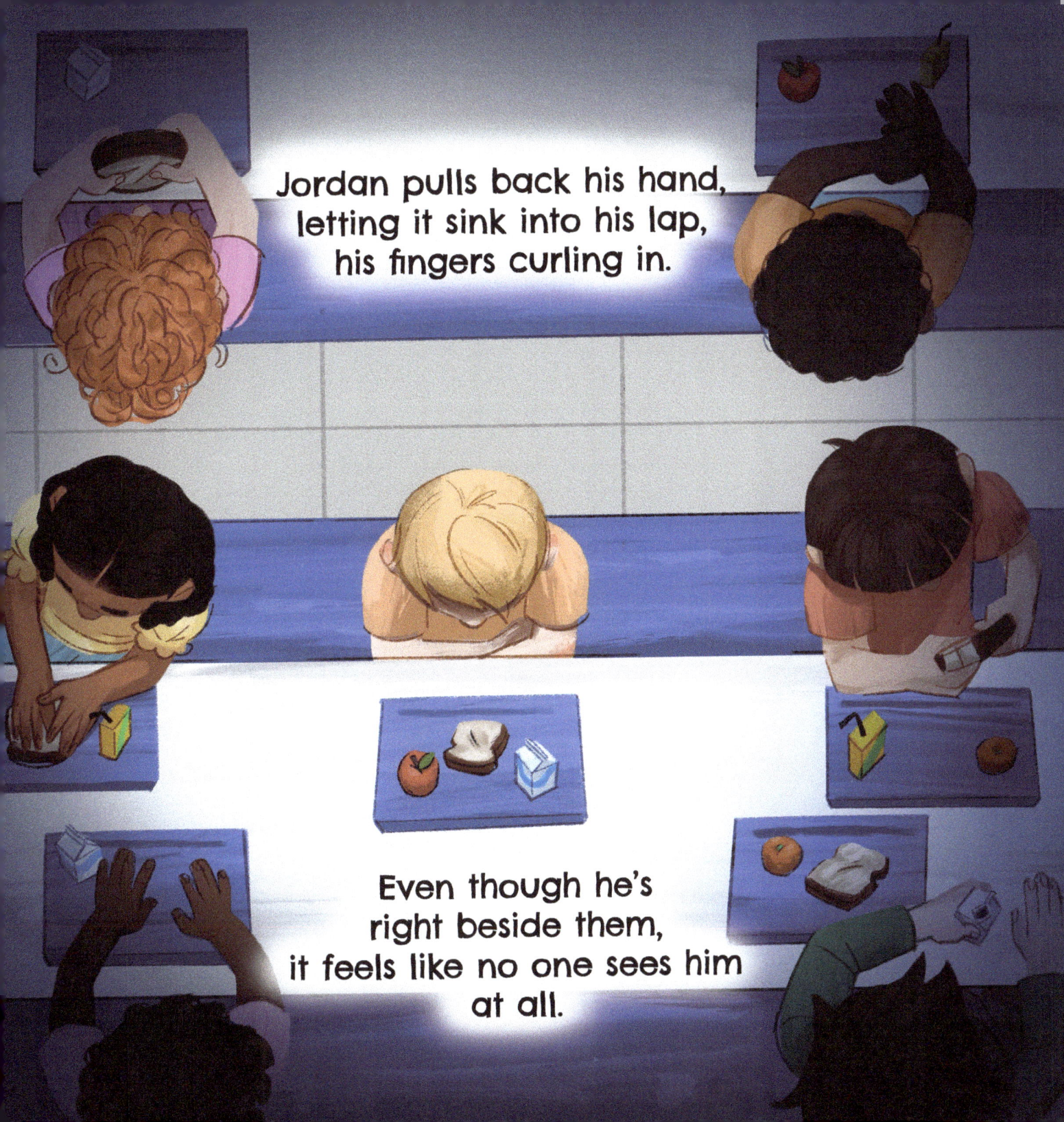

Jordan pulls back his hand,
letting it sink into his lap,
his fingers curling in.

Even though he's
right beside them,
it feels like no one sees him
at all.

Looking out the cafeteria doors, wanting to give up on making a friend, he wonders if things will ever get better.

But then, as he walks into his next class, he spots a boy named Linwood sitting at his desk.

Linwood waves

and Jordan waves back.

Jordan walks up to Linwood
and tries to speak -

and Linwood listens patiently
without interrupting.

He doesn't rush Jordan,
he just waits.

And that's when Jordan knows -
Linwood cares about what he has to say.

Linwood then asks if he would like to play at recess, and Jordan quickly nods his head.

At recess, Jordan and Linwood run and laugh together.

Jordan's face lights up, showing Linwood just how much fun he's having.

He points to what he wants to play next.

From that moment on,
their friendship doesn't stop at recess.

Linwood comes over to Jordan's house,

where they jump on the trampoline
and race across the yard.

On field day, they run side-by-side -
laughing as others cheer them on.

When Jordan joins the soccer team, Linwood joins him.

Linwood doesn't just play with Jordan - he understands him.

With Linwood by his side,
Jordan doesn't feel as alone.

He doesn't need all the words -
just one true friend is enough.

True friends show you
the acceptance and love that you've always deserved —
reminding you to give that same kindness to yourself.

Thank you to my childhood friend, Linwood,
for being the friend I needed.

Author Biography

Jordan Christian LeVan is a disability, mental health, and Individualized Education Plan (IEP) advocate based in Greensboro, North Carolina. He holds a Bachelor of Arts in Psychology with an emphasis on mental health studies and a minor in General Biology.

Additionally, he is certified in Orton-Gillingham instruction from the Orton-Gillingham Academy. Jordan is the lead advocate of Fighting for My Voice LLC, Founder & President of The Apraxia Foundation, and a managing partner of Camp Building Empowered Expression (BEE).

As the author of Jordan's World and Jordan's Journeys, he shares his real-life experiences to foster a more accepting and inclusive world.

www.ingramcontent.com/pod-product-compliance
Lightning Source LLC
Chambersburg PA
CBHW041127120626
46547CB00019B/2889